Starting Secondary School

Maths

by

Steve Mills and

Hilary Koll

Text and illustrations © Hodder Murray 2004

First published in 2004
exclusively for WHSmith
by Hodder Murray, a member of the Hodder Headline Group
338 Euston Road
London NW1 3BH

Impression number   5 4 3 2
Year   2008 2007 2006

Text: Steve Mills and Hilary Koll
Typeset by Fakenham Photosetting Ltd, Fakenham, Norfolk
Printed and bound in Spain

A CIP catalogue record for this book is available from the British Library

ISBN – 10   0 340 88741 9
ISBN – 13   978 0340 88741 7

Contents

Introduction

The move from primary to secondary school can be quite an overwhelming experience. You will encounter completely new subject areas and a whole range of new topics and concepts, as well as new teachers and a new and much bigger school environment. Some people say it is like changing from being a big fish in a small pond (primary school) to being a small fish in a big pond (secondary school)!

The books in this *Starting Secondary School* series will help bridge the gap between primary and secondary school and ease the transition between the two.

 **From a big fish in a small pond to a small fish in a big pond.**

This introduction will answer some of the most frequently asked questions about starting secondary school.

? What are lessons like at secondary school?

You'll probably be placed in a tutor group, which meets for registration each day with the same teacher, and you are likely to stay with this group for quite a few subjects. In some subjects, like English and maths, you may be placed in a set with other children of similar ability to make it easier for everyone in the set to work at a similar pace.

The timetable is very important at secondary school. Lessons are for set times and there may be a bell signalling the end of each lesson. Different subjects are taught in different rooms and you will be told and shown where to go. It is important to get to know your timetable as quickly as possible and to know where to go for each lesson. You could fill in the blank timetable at the end of this book to help you.

? Will I be able to find my way around?

Life at secondary school may seem very different to life at primary school at first. For a start, everything seems much bigger. The buildings are bigger, the students are bigger – and there are more of them! A common fear is of getting lost or not being able to find your way around. Don't worry. Your teachers will make sure you know where to go and there's always someone you can ask. Remember – if in doubt about anything, ask! Nobody will mind if you do. Everyone at the school is there to help you, and to help you to do your best.

? How do secondary schools work?

Each subject follows a scheme of work, which has been agreed by each subject department and will be based on Key Stage 3 of the National Curriculum. You will mostly study the same subjects you did at primary school. The main difference is that you will have different teachers to help you. You will also begin to study at least one modern foreign language, usually French or German. The choice of languages available differs from school to school.

? What about tests?

It is likely that you will have more tests and assessments at secondary school than you did at primary school. You will usually be told when these are to take place and will be given plenty of time to revise and prepare for them. If you are sensible and do your homework, these tests should not worry you at all.

? What about homework?

Homework is set in accordance with an agreed timetable so that you will have different subjects to deal with on different evenings. In your first year this will not be too time-consuming. A good tip is to do your homework as soon as you can, rather than leave it until the last minute and rush it. And remember to take it to school with you on the day you are supposed to hand it in!

? How will I cope with the extra freedom that I will have at secondary school?

A lot of emphasis is placed on being independent and responsible in secondary school. Thinking ahead and being organised will help you a lot. Always get to your lessons on time and take everything you need with you. The teachers will tell you what you need to bring to each lesson.

? How will my parents know what I am doing at school?

Most schools use a homework diary in which homework is recorded and some schools ask parents to sign this regularly to show that they have read it. It is important that your parents know what you are doing at school. This is one way of helping them find out. Don't forget to talk to them too! Your school will probably also have regular open evenings when your parents will be invited to school to talk to your teachers and discuss your progress.

? What will maths be like at secondary school?

At primary school you will have been familiar with maths largely being taught during the Daily Maths Lesson (sometimes called the Numeracy Hour). At secondary school you will study many of the same sorts of things at an appropriate level.

- You will learn number facts and use them to find out other facts.
- You will continue to learn about calculating, using mental and written methods.
- You will be expected to show your working.
- You will study the topics of fractions, decimals and percentages and how they relate to each other.
- You will be taught about topics, including algebra and transformations.
- You will be expected to solve problems within a range of different maths topics.

? How will this book help me?

All of the things in this book are designed to help you with work you will be doing at secondary school in maths. Work through the units in any order you wish. In the Glossary at the back of this book there is a list of useful words used in maths and their definitions.

Good luck!

Rounding

? Why do we round numbers?

If you look in newspapers you'll often see numbers that have been rounded. It makes a better headline to say

'MAN WINS A MILLION POUNDS!'

than

'MAN WINS NINE HUNDRED THOUSAND, SEVEN HUNDRED POUNDS AND TWELVE PENCE!'

Rounding helps us to calculate rough answers too...

411 × 19 is
about 400 × 20 = 8000

Maths words

The words 'rounding' or 'approximating' in maths are usually followed by the words 'to the nearest...'

People use **rounding** to change an exact number to an approximate (or rough) one.

To round numbers you must decide what you are rounding <u>to</u>.

This number	**55189**	
could be rounded to ...	**55190**	(to the nearest 10)
or to	**55200**	(to the nearest 100)
or to	**55000**	(to the nearest 1000)
or to	**60000**	(to the nearest 10000)

How do we round?

There are two main ways of rounding. Here is an instruction:

Round 55189 to the nearest 100.

One way is to look at the number and see which multiple of **100** the number is nearest to.

55100   55189 **55200**

It is nearest to 55200

The second way is this:
1. Firstly see what you are rounding to ...

Round 55189 to the nearest 100.

2. Then point to this digit in the number ...

TTh	Th	H	T	U
5	5	**1**	8	9

3. Now look at the digit to the right of it ...

5	5	**1**	8	9

4. If this is smaller than **5**, your digit stays the same. If it is **5** or larger your digit must go up one. Zeros then cover the digits to the right.

5	5	**2**	**0**	**0**

Examples

Round 4 967 230 to the nearest 1000.

M	HTh	Tth	Th	H	T	U
4	9	6	**7**	2	3	0

Point to 1000 digit.
Look to the right.
2 is less than 5.
So the digit 7 stays the same. Zeros cover the digits to the right.

4 967 000

Round 8 251 879 to the nearest 100.

M	HTh	Tth	Th	H	T	U
8	2	5	1	**8**	7	9

Point to 100 digit.
Look to the right.
7 is more than 5.
So the digit 8 needs to go up one. Zeros cover the digits to the right.

8 251 900

One more thing...
If your digit is a **9** and it needs to go up one, you have to change it to zero and add one to the digit on its left instead!
When rounding this number to the nearest **1000**...

8 2 5 9 8 7 9

becomes   8 2 6 0 0 0 0

Watch out when rounding this to the nearest **100**!

Try it yourself ▼

Round these numbers to the nearest 10, then to the nearest 100, then to the nearest 1000.

36842	76729	45971
5 748 551	9 409 852	2 659 968

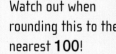

Did you know...?

We round decimals in exactly the same way. This time, though, numbers are rounded to the nearest... whole number, tenth, hundredth or thousandth, etc.
Look at this...
Round 93.684 to the nearest tenth.
Point to the tenths digit...

T U . t h th
9 3 . **6** 8 4

As 8 is larger than 5 we round the 6 up one, so the answer is...

9 3 . 7 0 0

We don't need to write the zeros at the end of a decimal so the answer is
9 3 . 7

More maths words

Sometimes we use the words **'decimal place'** instead of saying tenths, hundredths or thousandths, etc.
'Rounding to **1** decimal place' is the same as rounding to the nearest tenth.
'Rounding to **2** decimal places' is the same as rounding to the nearest hundredth and so on.

Negative numbers

? When do we use negative numbers?

Temperature is usually measured in degrees Celsius (°C). The temperature at which water freezes is 0 °C and any temperature colder than this we describe using negative numbers, such as −5 °C, −3 °C or −16 °C.

Maths words

'Positive numbers' are the numbers we normally use all the time, such as 4, 27 and 169. We <u>could</u> write them with a plus sign in front like this
+4, +27, +169
but we don't usually need to.
'Negative numbers' and **'positive numbers'** together are sometimes called **'directed numbers'**.

Negative numbers are numbers less than zero, like −4, −6.4, −8.333 and −19.

In maths, in years 6 and 7, we learn to order, add and subtract negative whole numbers.
A number line can help us do this . . .

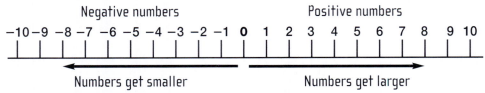

Negative numbers | Positive numbers

−10 −9 −8 −7 −6 −5 −4 −3 −2 −1 0 1 2 3 4 5 6 7 8 9 10

Numbers get smaller   Numbers get larger

When ordering numbers . . .

Remember, with negative numbers . . . **−10** is <u>smaller</u> than **−9**
even though, with positive numbers . . . **10** is <u>larger</u> than **9**
Always look at the number line to check!

Fill in the $<$ or $>$ signs to show which is larger or smaller.

−8 $<$ 0   0 ◯ −1   3 ◯ −5

−6 ◯ −1   −10 ◯ −9   −8 ◯ −5

−3 ◯ −4   −1 ◯ 1   −7 ◯ −9

When adding numbers, count along the number line towards the right . . .

−10 + 2 =   (answer is −8)

Point to this on the line   move to the **right**   two places

−6 + 9 = ☐   −9 + 4 = ☐   −3 + 8 = ☐

−4 + 7 = ☐   −2 + 5 = ☐   −1 + 11 = ☐

When subtracting numbers, count along the number line towards the left . . .

$$-6 - 3 = \qquad \text{(answer is } -9)$$

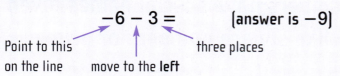

Point to this on the line   move to the **left**   three places

$-6 - 2 = \boxed{}$ $0 - 4 = \boxed{}$ $1 - 8 = \boxed{}$

$-1 - 3 = \boxed{}$ $-7 - 2 = \boxed{}$ $-3 - 7 = \boxed{}$

Sometimes, when you are adding and subtracting, two signs appear next to each other, like these...

$$1 - -3 = \qquad\qquad -3 + -4 =$$

subtraction sign   the number -3 addition sign   the number -4

If this happens, there are some rules you can follow to make it easier . . .

> $- \; -$ think of as a $+$
> $+ \; -$ think of as a $-$

So . . .

	$1 - -3 =$ and	$-3 + -4 =$
become	$1 + 3 = 4$ and	$-3 - 4 = -7$

Try it yourself

$-6 - -2 = \boxed{}$ $0 - -4 = \boxed{}$ $1 - -8 = \boxed{}$

$-1 + -4 = \boxed{}$ $-7 + -2 = \boxed{}$ $-5 + -3 = \boxed{}$

$-8 - -2 = \boxed{}$ $-1 + -4 = \boxed{}$ $-10 - -8 = \boxed{}$

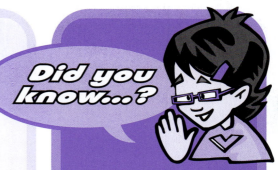

Did you know...?

In 1981 the temperature in the Kalahari Desert fell to $-5\,°C$. It even snowed! Vostok, a place in Antarctica, has an average annual temperature of $-57\,°C$!

⭐ **Temperature changes**

Do you know how to work out a new temperature if you are told by how much it has risen or fallen?
The temperature was $-5\,°C$. It rises by $8\,°C$. What is the new temperature?
Think of this as

$$-5 + 8 = $$

use addition for temperatures rising.
The temperature was $2\,°C$. It falls by $9\,°C$. What is the new temperature?
Think of this as

$$2 - 9 = $$

use subtraction for temperatures falling.

Squares, roots and primes

Some numbers have special names given to them like square numbers or prime numbers.

Square numbers are any numbers that have been made by multiplying a number by itself once.

1, 4, 9, 16, 25, 36, 49, 64, 81, 100 are all square numbers.

$1 = 1 \times 1$ $4 = 2 \times 2$ $9 = 3 \times 3$ $16 = 4 \times 4$
$25 = 5 \times 5$ $36 = 6 \times 6$ and so on

To square a number we multiply it by itself.
3 squared means 3×3 and is written as 3^2.
Find the answers to these questions:

5 squared = ☐ $4 \times 4 =$ ☐

$6^2 =$ ☐ $8^2 =$ ☐ $9^2 =$ ☐

The opposite of squaring a number is finding the square root.
This is the square root sign. $\sqrt{}$

The square root of the number 196 is written as $\sqrt{196}$.

To find it we use the $\boxed{\sqrt{}}$ key on the calculator.

   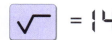

This tells us that 14×14 or 14^2 equals 196.

? **Why are they called square numbers?**
Square numbers can always be drawn as a series of dots making up a square. Look at this . . .

4   9   16

? **Did you know . . . ?**
In **1674** Gottfried von Leibniz, who became a famous mathematician, made a machine that is thought to be the very first calculator. It could add, subtract, multiply and divide and even find square roots!

! **Watch out!**
Check your calculator instruction book if you don't get this answer. You might have to press the square root key before the number.

I want to find which number has been multiplied by itself to give a square number. This is the square root.

Factors and prime numbers

Factors are whole numbers that divide exactly into another number without a remainder.

> The factors of **24** are **1, 2, 3, 4, 6, 8, 12, 24** as all these numbers divide into 24 without a remainder.

Prime numbers are whole numbers that have only two factors, the number itself and **1**.

> **17** is a prime number as **1 and 17** are the only numbers that divide into 17 without a remainder.

> To find out whether a number divides exactly into another without a remainder, use these simple tests:

If a number ends in **0, 2, 4, 6** or **8** it has the factor **2**
If a number ends in **0** or **5** it has the factor **5**
If a number ends in **0**, it has the factor **10**
If the sum of its digits is divisible by **9**, it has the factor **9**
If the sum of its digits is divisible by **3, 6** or **9**, it has the factor **3**
If it's even and it is divisible by **3**, it has the factor **6**
If, when halved, the answer is even, it has the factor **4**
If, when halved and halved again the answer is even, it has the factor **8**

Try it yourself

Use the list above to help you find the factors of these numbers between 1 and 10.

801	144	31	120

Which of these numbers is:

a prime number? _____   a square number? _____

Maths words

A **multiple** of a number is any number into which it will divide exactly, without a remainder.

> 15 has the **factors** 1, 3, 5 and 15.
>
> 15 is a **multiple** of 1, 3, 5 and 15.

Factors of square numbers

Square numbers always have an **odd** number of factors.

> 25 has the factors 1, 5 and 25.
> 16 has the factors 1, 2, 4, 8 and 16.
> 36 has the factors 1, 2, 3, 4, 6, 9, 12, 18, 36.

> To find the sum of the digits of a number just add them, like this . . .

385 sum of digits $= 3 + 8 + 5 = 16$
198 sum of digits $= 1 + 9 + 8 = 18$
104 sum of digits $= 1 + 0 + 4 = 5$

Use the square root key on your calculator.

Fractions

Sometimes we use a fraction wall to help us compare the sizes of fractions, like this...

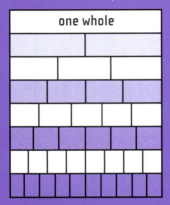

Each strip is one whole. Can you see that $\frac{2}{3}$ is the same as $\frac{4}{6}$?

 WISE UP

Another easy way to compare fractions is to make sure both fractions have the same denominator, like $\frac{3}{8}$ and $\frac{5}{8}$. It's easy to see which is larger!

Maths words

Equivalent fractions have the same value even though they have different **numerators** (top numbers) and **denominators** (bottom numbers).

A fraction is part of something that has been split into equal parts.

Fractions are written using two numbers, one on top of the other, like this...

5 ← The top number (the numerator) shows how many of the equal parts we are talking about.

8 ← The bottom number (the denominator) shows how many equal parts the whole has been split into.

Equivalent fractions

Fractions sometimes look very different but actually have the same value!

 $\frac{2}{3}$ $\frac{4}{6}$

To see if two fractions are equivalent, see if you can multiply the **numerator** and the **denominator** of one fraction by the **same number** to make the other fraction, like this...

$$\frac{2}{3} \xrightarrow{\times 2} \frac{4}{6}$$

These are equivalent.

(We could also <u>divide</u> the numerator and the denominator by the same number if necessary.)

So, to change a fraction to an equivalent one we can multiply or divide by any number we like ... As long as we do the <u>same</u> to the numerator as we do to the denominator!

$$\frac{1}{9} \xrightarrow{\times 5} \frac{5}{45} \qquad \frac{3}{9} \xrightarrow{\div 3} \frac{1}{3} \qquad \frac{400}{700} \xrightarrow{\div 100} \frac{4}{7}$$

When we divide by the largest number we can, and can't divide again by any other number, we say we have cancelled the fraction to its **simplest (or lowest) form**.

Adding and subtracting

To add and subtract fractions...

It's easy to add and subtract fractions with the same denominator, like this...

$$\frac{1}{8} + \frac{5}{8} = \frac{6}{8}$$ Notice that you don't add the denominators!

For an even better answer we can change it to its simplest form, like this...

$$\frac{6}{8} \xrightarrow{\div 2} \frac{3}{4}$$
$$\underset{\div 2}{}$$

But what if the denominators are NOT the same?
That's simple! Change them so that they are.

$$\frac{5}{6} - \frac{2}{3} =$$

$$\frac{2}{3} \xrightarrow{\times 2} \frac{4}{6}$$
$$\underset{\times 2}{}$$

$$\frac{5}{6} - \frac{4}{6} = \frac{1}{6}$$

Try it yourself ▼

Fill in the missing numbers to show equivalent fractions.

$$\frac{1}{3} = \frac{\square}{9} \qquad \frac{2}{4} = \frac{\square}{16} \qquad \frac{4}{5} = \frac{8}{\square}$$

$$\frac{5}{15} = \frac{\square}{3} \qquad \frac{12}{24} = \frac{1}{\square} \qquad \frac{6}{18} = \frac{1}{\square}$$

Now try adding and subtracting...

$$\frac{1}{7} + \frac{4}{7} = \square \qquad \frac{9}{10} - \frac{3}{10} = \square$$

$$\frac{5}{8} + \frac{1}{4} = \square \qquad \frac{2}{5} - \frac{3}{10} = \square$$

$$\frac{1}{3} + \frac{4}{9} = \square \qquad \frac{3}{5} - \frac{2}{15} = \square$$

> Can you change this answer to its simplest form?

Did you know...?

Did you know that some division questions have fractions as answers?

3 ÷ 4

could be thought of as 3 cakes shared between 4 people.

So $3 \div 4 = \frac{3}{4}$

What do you notice?

Yes, any fraction can be thought of as a division question!

$\frac{5}{9}$ is the same as $5 \div 9$

⚠ Fractions and decimals

To convert a fraction to a decimal, you can use a calculator. Just remember that a fraction can be thought of as a division.

$$\frac{5}{8}$$ [5] [÷] [8] [=]

$\frac{5}{8}$ as a decimal is 0.625

Decimals

? Why do we use decimals?

Decimals are easier to use than fractions because they work like whole numbers.

With <u>whole numbers</u>...

Th H T U . t h th

10 units make 1 ten,
10 tens make 1 hundred,
10 hundreds make
1 thousand and so on.

With <u>decimals</u>...

Th H T U . t h th

10 thousandths make
1 hundredth,
10 hundredths make
1 tenth, 10 tenths make
1 unit and so on.

This makes it very easy to add, subtract, multiply and divide decimals!

Maths words

The 'decimal point' is the dot separating the whole numbers from the part numbers.

Decimals, like fractions, are part numbers because they include amounts that are less than **1**, such as 0.5, 2.58 and 176.333.

Working with decimals you need to know what each digit in the number stands for.

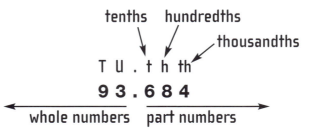

tenths   hundredths   thousandths

T U . t h th

9 3 . 6 8 4

whole numbers ← → part numbers

The numbers to the left of the decimal point show how many whole numbers we have. The numbers to the right show us how many tenths, hundredths, thousandths, etc. we have.

A tenth is the same as the fraction $\dfrac{1}{10}$

A hundredth is the same as $\dfrac{1}{100}$

and so on.

So 0.61 means 6 tenths and 1 hundredth

or 61 hundredths $\dfrac{61}{100}$

Fill in the missing numbers to show the decimals as fractions.

tenths

$0.3 = \dfrac{}{10}$

hundredths

$0.04 = \dfrac{}{100}$

$0.47 = \dfrac{}{100}$

$0.5 = \dfrac{}{}$

Can you change this answer to its simplest form?

$0.25 = \dfrac{}{}$

Can you change this answer to its simplest form?

$6.41 = \mathbf{6}\dfrac{}{100}$

This is a mixed number with a whole number and a fraction.

Ordering decimals

It's important to realise that tenths are larger than hundredths, and hundredths are larger than thousandths, and so on.

 0.4 is larger than **0.04**

 0.4 is larger than **0.38**

Just because this number has 2 digits after the decimal point it does not necessarily mean it is larger.
Look to see how many tenths it has first!

You could think of **0.4** as **0.40** where the zero shows it has no hundredths. It is easier to compare **0.40** with **0.38** as they have the same number of digits after the decimal point.

Example

Put these in order, smallest first.
0.4821   0.576   0.58   0.6   0.581

1. All the numbers have no whole ones.
   Look at the tenths digits.
   The smallest number has **4** tenths.

2. Then there are three numbers with **5** tenths.
   0.576   0.58   0.581
   Look at the hundredths digits for these.
   The smallest of these has **5** tenths and **7** hundredths.

3. The other two both have 8 hundredths.
   0.58   0.581
   Look at the thousandths digits for these. The smaller has 5 tenths, 8 hundredths and **0** thousandths.

4. So the next one will be . . .

5. Leaving the largest one of all with **6** tenths.

> **0.4**821
>
> **0.5**76
>
> **0.58**0
>
> **0.58**1
>
> **0.6**

Try it yourself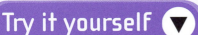

Put these in order, smallest first.

0.836   0.841   0.9   0.7806   0.84

Decimals on a number line

Between each whole number on a number line lie decimals (or fractions).
Between 2 and 3 lie decimals such as
2.5, 2.99, 2.345.
Between 2.5 and 2.6 lie decimals such as
2.51, 2.52, 2.586.
Can you name some decimals that lie between 3.6 and 3.7?

Maths words

Sometimes we use the words **decimal place** to tell us how many digits are after the decimal point.
1 decimal place means **one digit** after the decimal point.
2 decimal places mean **two digits** after the decimal point and so on . . .
How many decimal places has each of these?

0.9
7.7806
300.842
36.5

Try this . . .

How many different numbers can you make with these cards?

Make decimals with 1 decimal place, 2 decimal places and 3 decimal places.
Try putting the numbers you have made in order.

Percentages

? Why do we use percentages?

Percentages help us to compare things. For example, Joe took three tests and these are his results:

6	15	13
10	25	20

In which test did he do best?

To find out, we change each of these to a percentage.

In the first two tests he scored 60%, in the third he scored 65%.

To learn how to do this read the rest of the page!

! Reminder!

To find a fraction of a number, divide the number by the **denominator** and multiply it by the **numerator**.

Example:

To find $\frac{3}{4}$ of a number, divide it by **4** (to find $\frac{1}{4}$) and multiply by **3**.

A **percentage** is a fraction with a denominator of 100, but written in a different way. We write 72% to mean $\frac{72}{100}$.

Percentages, fractions and decimals like those below are all related.

25%, $\frac{25}{100}$ and 0.25 all have the same value.

Per cent means out of a hundred.

We say this is 'twenty five per cent' or 'twenty five out of a hundred'.

These also have the same value. Can you see why?

25%, $\frac{1}{4}$ and 0.25.

(Look back to page 12 to find out more about equivalent fractions if you need to.)

To find a percentage of a number...

It is often easier to think of the percentage as a fraction and then to change it to its simplest form.

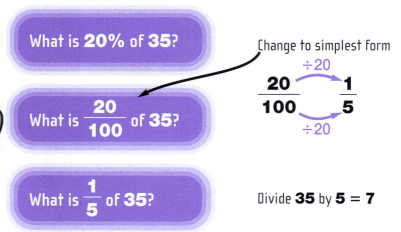

What is **20%** of **35**?

What is $\frac{20}{100}$ of **35**?

What is $\frac{1}{5}$ of **35**?

Change to simplest form

$$\frac{20}{100} \xrightarrow[\div 20]{\div 20} \frac{1}{5}$$

Divide **35** by **5** = **7**

So **20% of 35 = 7**

Try answering these questions, by changing the percentage to a fraction and then to its simplest form.

What is:

20% of **300**?	**25%** of **300**?	**75%** of **24**?
10% of **960**?	**40%** of **300**?	**30%** of **60**?

Percentages on a number line

These number lines show how percentages, decimals and fractions are related.

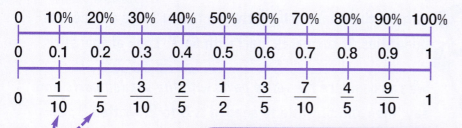

All the fractions have been changed to an equivalent fraction in its simplest form.

To convert a percentage to a decimal just divide by 100.
$60\% = 60 \div 100 = 0.6$
$42\% = 42 \div 100 = 0.42$

Comparing fractions using percentages

Convert each to a fraction with a denominator of 100.

$$\frac{6}{10} \xrightarrow[\times 10]{\times 10} \frac{60}{100} = 60\%$$

$$\boxed{\frac{6}{10}} \quad \boxed{\frac{15}{25}} \quad \boxed{\frac{13}{20}}$$

$$\frac{15}{25} \xrightarrow[\times 4]{\times 4} \frac{60}{100} = 60\%$$

$$\frac{13}{20} \xrightarrow[\times 5]{\times 5} \frac{65}{100} = 65\%$$

If you were using a calculator you could divide the numerator by the denominator to get a decimal and then multiply by **100** to get the percentage.

Try these...

Compare the three fractions in each set by converting them to percentages.

$\frac{2}{5}$	$\frac{4}{10}$	$\frac{21}{50}$

$\frac{4}{10}$	$\frac{9}{25}$	$\frac{7}{20}$

$\frac{1}{5}$	$\frac{6}{25}$	$\frac{5}{20}$

$\frac{4}{5}$	$\frac{19}{25}$	$\frac{17}{20}$

Did you know...?
About 70% of the Earth's surface is covered in water!

Asia is the largest of the seven continents – it covers about 30% of all the land on Earth.
Over 80% of the people in the world live in the Northern Hemisphere.

For more on multiplying and dividing by **100** see page 23.

Maths words

'Per cent' means 'out of every hundred' or 'for every hundred'.

'Converting' means changing something from one form to another, such as changing percentages to fractions or decimals.

Ratio and proportion

? Why do we use ratio and proportion?

Ratio and proportion help us to compare things. For example, if Joe has £4 and Rob has £1 . . .

the ratio is 4 to 1, written **4 : 1**, where Joe has 4 'parts' and Rob has one 'part'.

The proportion of the total Joe has is 4 parts out of 5, written as
$\frac{4}{5}$, **0.8** or **80%**.
Rob has 1 out of 5. His proportion is 1 part out of 5, written as
$\frac{1}{5}$, **0.2** or **20%**

Maths words
Simplifying a ratio makes it easier to work with.
When we have simplified a ratio as much as possible, it is in its simplest form, for example, 5:1, 7:2 and 9:5.

Ratio and **proportion** are used to compare numbers or quantities.

Ratio is the relationship between two or more numbers or quantities. It compares 'part with part'. Look at this stick:

We can compare *the white parts with the shaded parts* and say 'the ratio of white to shaded is 3 to 2, written 3 : 2.

Proportion is the relationship between part of something and the whole thing. It compares 'part with whole'.

We can compare *the white parts with the whole stick* and say 'the proportion of white parts is 3 out of 5'.

We can write this as $\frac{3}{5}$, 0.6 or 60%.

When working with ratios . . .
We can multiply the numbers in the ratio and the relationship is still the same.

$\times 3 \overset{4:1}{\underset{12:3}{}} \times 3$ $\times 10 \overset{4:1}{\underset{40:10}{}} \times 10$

We can also **simplify** a ratio by dividing both numbers in the same way.

$\div 5 \overset{4:1}{\underset{20:5}{}} \div 5$ $\div 7 \overset{5:2}{\underset{35:14}{}} \div 7$

In other words, we can make the numbers in a ratio easier to work with, but the ratio stays the same.

Simplify these ratios:

| 10:2 | 15:3 | 20:10 | 20:4 |
| 100:25 | 16:8 | 25:5 | 39:13 |

We can also simplify proportions by finding equivalent fractions, so the proportion $\frac{8}{10}$ can become $\frac{4}{5}$. Look for more on equivalent fractions on page 12.

Working with ratio and proportion

Write the answers to these in their simplest form.

Choc crispies

chocolate	60 g
crispies	10 g

What proportion of the choc crispies is chocolate?

What is the ratio of chocolate to crispies?

Raspberry jam

raspberries	180 g
sugar	90 g

What proportion of the jam is raspberries?

What is the ratio of raspberries to sugar?

Blackcurrant drink

water	1500 ml
blackcurrant	300 ml

What proportion of the drink is water?

What is the ratio of water to blackcurrant?

Examples

Cheese pie for 3 people
Cheese 600 g
Butter 60 g
Pastry 180 g
If I want to make cheese pie for 2 people, how much cheese is needed?

Find how much cheese is needed for one person by dividing 600 by 3.
Each person needs 200 g.
Double this to find how much is needed for two people.
Answer: **400** g

There are **28** students in a class in the ratio **3** boys to every **4** girls, or in the ratio **3 : 4**.

How many girls are there?

Find the proportion of the class that is girls by adding the numbers in the ratio: $3 + 4 = 7$

$\frac{4}{7}$ of the class are girls.

$\frac{1}{7}$ of 28 is 4 and so $\frac{4}{7}$ is 16

Answer: **16** girls

What to do
Write $\frac{60}{70}$ and then change to its simplest form.

Write 60 : 10 and then change to its simplest form.

⊛ Working to scale
Look at the scales on maps. Can you work out what they mean?
For example, you might be studying a map which has the scale **1 : 10 000** or **1 : 25 000** written at the side.
This means each distance on the map is, in real life, 10 000 times or 25 000 times longer than on the map.

❗ Try this ...
Deepa went running. She jogged then sprinted in the ratio 7 : 2.
If she ran 1800 m in total, how far did she jog?
Start by finding the total of the ratio by adding the two numbers together.
How many times larger is the distance she ran?
Multiply the 'jogging' number in the ratio by this number to find the answer.

Number facts

Doubling
Use partitioning to help you double.

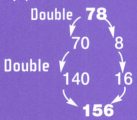

Double **78**
70   8
Double
140   16
156

⭐ Using known facts
If you find it hard to learn facts off by heart then try to use any facts you do know to help you answer new facts, like this...

I know that double 45 is 90.

This means that Jimmy can also answer any of these questions

45 × 2	90 ÷ 2
half of 90	45 + 46
44 + 45	90 − 45
90 − 46	90 − 44
double 4.5	double 450
double 0.45	
half of 9000	half of 0.9

and many more like this!

Halving
Use partitioning to help you halve.

Halve **74**
70   4
Halve
35   2
37

There are many number facts that you should know by heart or be able to work out quickly. How well do you know these?

DOUBLES – Test yourself

Double each number.

26	37	49	74
3.9	4.5	7.2	0.54
0.63	0.38	480	650
790	4600	8200	94000

HALVES – Test yourself

Halve each number.

52	84	96	68
8.2	6.8	7.4	0.88
0.92	0.76	480	640
780	4600	8200	94000

Remember to use facts you know already to help you.

$$38 + 38 = 76$$

$$380 + 380 = 760 \quad \text{numbers } 10 \text{ times larger}$$
$$3800 + 3800 = 7600 \quad \text{numbers } 100 \text{ times larger}$$
$$38000 + 38000 = 76000 \quad \text{numbers } 1000 \text{ times larger}$$

$$3.8 + 3.8 = 7.6 \quad \text{numbers } 10 \text{ times smaller}$$
$$0.38 + 0.38 = 0.76 \quad \text{numbers } 100 \text{ times smaller}$$

How many different questions like this can you answer by changing the numbers in this fact to be **10**, **100** or **1000** times larger or smaller?
76 + 76 = 152

Multiplication and division facts

You need to know tables facts by heart

See how easily you can fill in the missing numbers in this multiplication square.

5×6

Do you know all the square numbers up to 12×12?

$1 \times 1 = 1$
$2 \times 2 = 4$
$3 \times 3 = 9$
$4 \times 4 = 16 \ldots$

$11 \times 11 = ?$
$12 \times 12 = ?$

×	6	7	8	9
5				
6				
7				
8				

See page **10** to find out more about square numbers.

Don't forget you can make these multiplications **10**, **100** or **1000** times larger or smaller . . .

$$7 \times 8 = 56$$

$70 \times 8 = 560$

$7 \times 80 = 560$

$70 \times 80 = 5600$

$7 \times 0.8 = 5.6$

$0.7 \times 8 = 5.6$

$0.7 \times 0.8 = 0.56$

Division facts

These are simply your multiplication tables facts in reverse . . .

$7 \times 8 = 56$
$56 \div 8 = 7$
$56 \div 7 = 8$

Try it yourself ▼

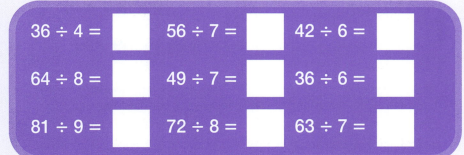

$36 \div 4 = \boxed{}$ $56 \div 7 = \boxed{}$ $42 \div 6 = \boxed{}$

$64 \div 8 = \boxed{}$ $49 \div 7 = \boxed{}$ $36 \div 6 = \boxed{}$

$81 \div 9 = \boxed{}$ $72 \div 8 = \boxed{}$ $63 \div 7 = \boxed{}$

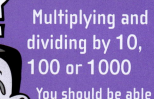

Multiplying and dividing by 10, 100 or 1000

You should be able to multiply or divide any number by 10, 100 or 1000, including decimals.

See page 23 for more information on how to do this.

We could write this as

$7 \times 8 \div \mathbf{10}$

and this as

$7 \times 8 \times \mathbf{100}$

Maths words

A number is exactly divisible by another if it can be divided into by this number without leaving a remainder, for example 25 is exactly divisible by 5.

See page 11 for how to find out whether a number is exactly divisible by another.

Calculations 1

Calculating with decimals

Decimals work in the same way as whole numbers. When you add or subtract decimals using a written method, just make sure that you arrange them so that the decimal points are in line, like this...

3.46 + 15.7 =

$$
\begin{array}{r}
3.46 \\
+\ 15.70 \\
\hline
19.16
\end{array}
$$

A zero (to show no hundredths) has been written to make it easier to line them up.

Always show your working out in a test as you might get a mark for it, even if you get the final answer wrong!

If you have been taught a different way to do these, don't worry! The important thing is that you can get to the correct answer in a way that you understand.

Calculations include addition, subtraction, multiplication and division. **To calculate** means to work something out.

You need to know how to calculate with whole numbers and decimals, in your head and on paper.

Remember the letters   A   C   C

Approximate first   then Calculate   then Check

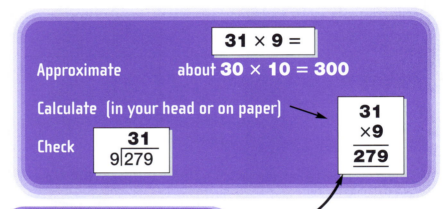

31 × 9 =

Approximate   about **30 × 10 = 300**

Calculate (in your head or on paper)

$$
\begin{array}{r}
31 \\
\times 9 \\
\hline
279
\end{array}
$$

Check
$$
\begin{array}{r}
31 \\
9\overline{)279}
\end{array}
$$

Different methods

There are lots of different ways of finding the answer to a question. Here are some common ones...

Multiplication

$$
\begin{array}{r}
127 \\
\times\ 35 \\
\hline
3810 \quad 127 \times 30 \\
635 \quad 127 \times 5 \\
\hline
4445
\end{array}
$$

Division

$$
\begin{array}{r}
189 \\
5\overline{)945} \\
\underline{500} \quad (100 \times 5) \\
445 \\
\underline{400} \quad (80 \times 5) \\
45 \\
\underline{45} \quad (9 \times 5) \\
0
\end{array}
$$

If you are asked to multiply or divide decimals, treat them like whole numbers. Use your approximation to help you decide where to put the decimal point in your answer.

Other calculations

Find **3.45 × 2.3**

Approximate $3 \times 2 = \mathbf{6}$

Calculate

```
   345
 ×  23
  6900    345 × 20
  1035    345 × 3
  7935
```

The answer must be **7.935** rather than 79.35 or 793.5 because our approximation was **6**.

Answer = **7.935**

Check   Use a different method or operation to check →

```
          345
     23)7935
          69
         103
          92
         115
         115
           0
```

Fractions

These all mean the same thing. Can you see why?

$\frac{1}{4}$ of **20**   **20** × $\frac{1}{4}$ $\frac{1}{4}$ × **20**   **20** ÷ **4** $\frac{20}{4}$

(Read more about fractions on page 12.)

Practise your calculation methods by solving this puzzle.
If you need to, write decimal points on the lines, like this...

```
2 . 4  5
```

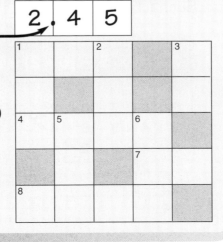

Across
1 13^2
4 321 × 4
7 $\sqrt{2500}$
8 183 × 23

Down
1 3000 − 2899
2 7.12 + 2.26
3 $\frac{1}{4}$ of 48
5 1048 ÷ 4
6 22.95 ÷ 5

⭐ **Multiplying and dividing by 10, 100 or 1000**

It's important to know what each digit in a number is worth.

Th H T U. t h th
      4 2. 3 5

When we multiply by 10 the digits move one place to the left.

When we divide by 10 the digits move one place to the right.

Th H T U. t h th
      4 2. 3 5   × 10
    4 2 3. 5

Th H T U. t h th
      4 2. 3 5   ÷ 10
      4. 2 3 5

When multiplying or dividing by **100** the digits move two places.

When multiplying or dividing by **1000** the digits move three places, and so on.

❗ Try these...

| **5.2** | **0.04** |

× 10, ÷ 10, × 100,
÷ 100, × 1000, ÷ 1000

Calculations 2

Working out!

Always show your working out in a test as you might get a mark for it, even if you get the final answer wrong!

Why do we use BODMAS?

If mathematicians hadn't agreed on an order to do calculations, everyone would get different answers!

Look at the different answers for this . . .

$$4 + 3 \times 5 - 1 =$$

Using BODMAS the answer is 18.

If we worked from left to right the answer would be 34.

Even an answer of 28 could be made if we did the subtraction first.

Imagine how confused we would all be if we hadn't agreed on an order.

ALWAYS USE THE ORDER OF **BODMAS!**

Even when you are doing **calculations** using a calculator, always follow the ACC steps.

Remember the letters   **A**   **C**   **C**

Approximate first   then Calculate   then Check

> The other thing you need to know is what order to key things into your calculator.

> Don't just key in the numbers from left to right. You might get the wrong answer. Use BODMAS to help you.

$$3 + 4 \times 5 - (6 + 2) + 2^2$$

BODMAS

The letters of this word help us to remember the agreed order in which to do calculations.

Brackets   (do anything in brackets first)

Other   (other things include squaring or finding the square root)

Divide
Multiply   (then divide or multiply numbers)

Add
Subtract   (and finally add or subtract numbers)

$$3 + 4 \times 5 - (6 + 2) \div 2^2$$

$3 + 4 \times 5 - 8 \div 2^2$
$3 + 4 \times 5 - 8 \div 4$
$3 + 4 \times 5 - 2$
$3 + 20 - 2$
$23 - 2$
21

So to answer this...
Brackets
Other
Divide
Multiply
Add
Subtract

1. $10 + 4 \times 2 + (20 + 7) \div 3^2$
2. $20 - (6 + 4) \div 5 - 4 \times 2^2$
3. $(2 + 10) + 15 \div 3 + 2 \times 5$
4. $(5 + 5) + 20 \div (4 + 1) + 4$

If any of the words in **BODMAS** don't appear in the calculation – don't worry – just keep going!

If you see a calculation written like a fraction, with some numbers beneath a line, this means that what is on top of the line is divided by what is on the bottom.

$$\frac{6 + 5 \times 2}{3 - 1}$$

means

$$(6 + 5 \times 2) \div (3 - 1)$$

Notice that when we rewrite it this way we include brackets.

Answer these questions using **BODMAS** and a calculator.

1. $\dfrac{6.9 + 5.4}{6.9 - 5.4}$ → $(6.9 + 5.4) \div (6.9 - 5.4)$

2. $\dfrac{3.1 + 4.7}{6 - 5.4}$

3. $\dfrac{4.5 - 3.7}{0.2 + 0.05}$

4. $\dfrac{13 - 0.3}{0.1 \times 3}$

42.33333333 means **42** and one third or $42\frac{1}{3}$

Calculators and money

Watch out when you are solving problems involving money on a calculator. For example, your calculator may show an answer of **4.8**, but you can't write this as your answer. If this is the number of pounds, you must write the answer **£4.80**.

Maths words

When we work with calculators we are sometimes asked to round the answer.
This might be . . .
to the nearest whole number
to **1** decimal place
(to the nearest tenth)
to **2** decimal places
(to the nearest hundredth)
and so on.
For more information on rounding see page 6.

Solving problems

See page 22 to find out more about ACC.

Problems, problems, problems...!

Problems in maths can involve understanding of any topic. If you don't understand the topic you won't be able to solve problems about it. If there are any problems on this page that you don't understand, look at the pages on these topics to see if they will give you a clue ...
Calculations, Ratio and proportion, Decimals.

Maths words

'Solve' means to find the answer or answers to the question.

Maths is only useful to you if you know how to **solve problems**.

There are different types of problems to solve:
Worded problems, puzzles and showing whether statements are true or false.

Worded problems

When solving worded problems, follow these steps:

1. First read the problem carefully right through to the end.
2. Write down the important numbers in the question and what they are (or draw them if it helps).
3. Decide what you will do to work it out.
4. Approximate, then Calculate, then Check. (ACC)

Example

Notice that when you add or subtract you must decide to work in pounds or in pence, not both!

> A drink and a burger together cost **90**p.
> A drink and two burgers together cost **£1.45**.
> What does the drink cost?

1. Read carefully.

2. = 90p

 = £1.45

3. If I subtract 90p from £1.45 I will find out the cost of one burger.
4. A burger must be about 50p.
145p − 90p = <u>55p</u>.   So if a drink + 55p = 90p
the drink must cost **35**p.
Check: 35p + 55p + 55p = 145p Correct!

Puzzles

There are many different types of mathematical puzzles.

Some puzzles may need to be broken down into smaller steps.

Try these puzzles:

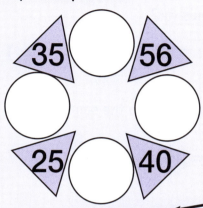

1. Write a number in each circle so that the number in each triangle is the product of the two numbers on either side of it.

2. Write the numbers **1** to **9** into these squares so that the total of each adjacent pair of numbers is **9**, **10** or **11**.

3. How many different ways can you arrange these four vases in a line?

Saying whether statements are true or false

If you can find one example that doesn't fit the statement then the statement is false.

All the numbers between 0 and 9 are written with only curved lines

1 is written with a straight line.

So this statement is false.

Can you find one example that doesn't fit these statements?

If not, the statement is likely to be true.

★ If you add three consecutive numbers the answer will always be odd.

★ All rectangles have four right angles.

★ All the numbers between **40** and **49** have only two digits.

More maths words

The **product** of two numbers is the answer when the two numbers are *multiplied* together.

Adjacent means next to each other.

Did you know...?

⭐ **It's good to talk!**

Sometimes it is easier to solve a problem by talking about it to someone. In Year 7 you will be given chances to work with a partner or in a small group. Be prepared to speak up and suggest your ideas. Other people in your group may not have thought of the problem in the same way as you.

Did you think about decimal numbers here?

Maths words

Number sentences, like these, are called 'equations' because they have an equals sign.
If there is no equals sign, such as y + **7**, they are called 'expressions'.

⊛ WISE UP

2n means 2 lots of n. It is the same as 2 × n or n × 2 or even n + n.

n/2 means n divided by 2. It is the same as n ÷ 2 or $\frac{1}{2}$ n.

Algebra is a part of maths where we use letters to stand for numbers.

These symbols are used in place of numbers. Can you work out what each stands for?

$$\triangle + 2 = 5 \qquad 19 - \bigcirc = 12 \qquad \square \times 2 = 3 + 1$$

Algebra uses letters in place of numbers in the same way. Work out what each letter stands for.

$$y + 7 = 10 \qquad 27 - b = 24 \qquad c - 15 = 21$$

> y stands for a number. When we add 7 to y we get 10. So y must stand for 3.

Here Danny has begun to write some puzzles in words. These can be written as expressions using any letter to stand for the number he is thinking of. Here, the letter n has been used.

I think of a number and add three to it.
n + 3

I think of a number and subtract six from it.
n − 6

I think of a number. I subtract this number from 9.
9 − n

I think of a number and double it.
2n

I think of a number. I multiply it by 2 and add one.
2n + 1

I think of a number, halve it and subtract four.
n/2 − 4

Solving equations

I think of a number. I multiply it by 2 and add one.

If the answer to Joshua's puzzle was **11**, what was the number he thought of?

I think of a number and add four. My answer is eighteen.

We can write the puzzle as the equation: $2n + 1 = 11$

To solve this we must find what n is.

★ first find **2**n ⟶ to what number do we add **1** to get **11**?
   so **2**n must equal **10**
★ then find n ⟶ if **2**n is **10** then n is half of **10**
★ so n = 5

HELPFUL HINT

Always check by putting your answer back into the equation.
$2n + 1 = 11$
2 lots of **5** is 10, then add 1. Does it equal 11?

Examples

I choose a card from a set of 0 to 9 cards. If I subtract 4 from the number on the card, the answer is 3. What number is on the card?

$$n - 4 = 3$$

Find n by saying, "What number can I subtract 4 from and get 3?".
So n = **7**

I am given £n for my birthday. If I add this to the £12 I got for Christmas I have £23. How much did I get for my birthday?

$$n + 12 = 23$$

Find n by saying, "What number can I add 12 to and get 23?".
So n = **11**

I have n goldfish in my fish tank. If I doubled the number of fish but then three died, I would have 7 fish. How many did I start with?

$$2n - 3 = 7$$

Find 2n by saying, "What number can I subtract 3 from and get 7?".
So 2n = **10** and n must be **5**.

? How does algebra help us?

Using letters or symbols can help us to explore number patterns and to solve puzzles and problems like this:

We can sometimes solve a puzzle more easily if we use algebra.

Let's call the number **n** (or any other letter you choose).

To what number do you add 4 to get 18?

So we can write this as
$n + 4 = 18$

n must stand for 14.

! Try it yourself

Think of a number. Add two, then add three, then subtract four and then subtract one. What do you notice about the answer? Try this for other start numbers.

Write the puzzle as an expression, using the letter n to stand for the first number. Can you see why the answer is always the same as the first number?

Algebra 2

A type of shorthand!

Mathematicians like to write things using a kind of shorthand.

Instead of writing 5 × a or a + a + a + a + a, they prefer to write 5a.

It's quicker!

Keep numbers on their own, separate from the letters.

When simplifying an expression with brackets, multiply <u>every</u> part in the brackets by the number outside.

Maths words

When we **simplify** we can collect together letters that are the same. This is sometimes called 'collecting like terms'.

In algebra, you must learn to **simplify** and **substitute**.

Simplifying

To **simplify** is to write in a simpler form.

Can you see how these have been simplified?

$a + a + a + a + a = 5a$ $2a + 4a + 2a = 8a$

$a + 2a + 6 = 3a + 6$ $a + 4 + a + 4 = 2a + 8$

Here are some other ways we can write expressions in a simpler form:

$\dfrac{a}{a} = 1$ $\dfrac{2a}{a} = 2$ $\dfrac{3a}{a} = 3$

$3(a + 5) = 3a + 15$ $6(2 + a) = 12 + 6a$

$a \times a = a^2$ $a \times a \times a = a^3$

Try these . . .

Simplify: $c + c + c + c$	Simplify: $g + 2g + 2g + g$	Simplify: $y + 2y + 3y + 7$
4c		

Simplify: $\dfrac{d}{d}$	Simplify: $4(f + 2)$	Simplify: $b \times b \times b$

Substituting

If you are substituted in a football match another player takes your place.

In algebra, if you substitute a number for a letter it means the number takes the place of the letter.

Substitute:

$x = 5$
$y = 2$
$z = 8$ → $x + y + z = 5 + 2 + 8 = 15$

$c = 3$
$d = 7$ → $2(c + d) = 2(3 + 7) = 20$

Substituting is particularly useful when we use a formula.
Here is the formula for working out the area of a rectangle.

length   width

Area $= l \times w$

$l = 100$ metres and $w = 70$ metres

To find the area we substitute the measurements for the letters in the formula, like this . . .
Area $= 100 \times 70 = 7000\,\text{m}^2$

Try it yourself ▼

If $a = 2$, $b = 3$ and $c = 4$, find the value of each expression.

$a + b + c$	$3(a + b)$	$a + c + 1$
$c + b - 2$	$c - b + a$	$3a + 1$
$c \div a$	$a \times b$	$4a + 2b$

? **How does substituting help us?**

People use formulae to help them in many different ways . . .
To work out how much fence a farmer needs to go around his field, he might use the formula
$2(l + w)$
where l is the length and w is the width of his field.
To work out how much interest to pay, a bank clerk might use the formula
$n \times 2.5 \div 100$
where n is the amount of money someone has.

For more about area see page 46.

One more thing . . .
3a means $3 \times a$, so when you substitute a number into the expression 3a remember to multiply the number by 3.

Sequences

Numbers arranged in a special order are called **sequences**. Sequences can be **ascending** or **descending**.

Sequences can increase or decrease by the same sized steps, like these...

$$1, 3, 5, 7, 9, 11 \dots \qquad 8, 6, 4, 2, 0, -2, -4 \dots$$

Or they can increase or decrease by different sized steps, like these...

$$1, 4, 9, 16, 25, 36 \dots \qquad 1, 2, 4, 8, 16, 32 \dots$$

Famous sequences

There are some sequences that you should learn to recognise, like these...

Square numbers
1, 4, 9, 16, 25, 36...
For more about these see page 10.

Triangular numbers
1, 3, 6, 10, 15, 21...

Position or term number
The rule must work for every term in the sequence.

It is important to be able to say which **term** you are talking about.

1, 4, 9, 16, 25, 36 ...

> The third term in this sequence is 9.

> The fifth term in this sequence is 25.

> I think the tenth term in this sequence will be 100.

Describing the rule for a sequence

There are two ways of describing sequences.

a) One way is to explain how each term is different from the previous term.

$$3, 7, 11, 15, 19, 23 \dots$$

> Each term is increasing by 4.

b) The other is to explain how you can work out each term from where it is in the sequence.

1 2 3 4 5 6
$$3, 7, 11, 15, 19, 23 \dots$$
$$3 \times 4 - 1 = 11 \qquad 5 \times 4 - 1 = 19$$
$$4 \times 4 - 1 = 15$$

> Multiply the position number by 4 and subtract 1.

Using rules

Sometimes rules are written using a letter to stand for where in the sequence a term is (its position).

These three rules are the same – can you see why?

Multiply the position number by **3** and add **1**	**n** × **3** + **1**
	3n + **1**

n is the position or term number.
We can write the sequence using any of these rules.

1. Write the positions in a line   **1 2 3 4 5 6**
2. Start with the first term, where
   the position number (or n) is **1** $1 \times 3 + 1 = 4$
3. Then the second term, where
   the position number (or n) is **2** $2 \times 3 + 1 = 7$
4. Then the third term, where
   the position number (or n) is **3** $3 \times 3 + 1 = 10$
   and so on . . .

                         1 2 3 4 5 6

Write the sequence in a line . . .   4   7   10 13 16 19 . . .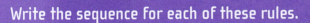

Try these . . .

Write the sequence for each of these rules.

Multiply the position number by **4** and add **1**	Multiply the position number by **5** and subtract **4**
n × **2** + **1**	**5n** − **1**

Can you **predict** what the **100**th term will be in each of the sequences above?

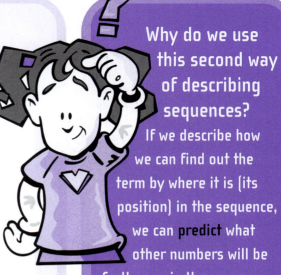

Why do we use this second way of describing sequences?
If we describe how we can find out the term by where it is (its position) in the sequence, we can **predict** what other numbers will be further on in the sequence. If I know that the rule for a sequence is

Multiply the position number by 3 and add 1

then I can **predict** that the 100th number in the sequence is 301!

Three dots at the end of a sequence show that the sequence goes on forever (towards **infinity**).

**4, 7, 10, 13, 16,
19,
22,
25,
28,
31,
34,
37,
40, 43, 46, 49, 52,
55,
58,
61,
64,
67,
70 . . .**

Functions

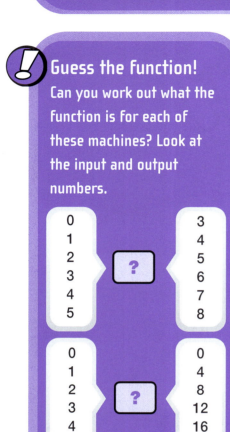
Did you know...?

Functions can be programmed into computer spreadsheets so that you don't have to work out each answer!

Functions are rules that we use on a set of numbers. Each number in the set will match up with only one answer.

Function machines can help us to understand functions more easily. Here we input each of these numbers: 1, 2, 3, 4, 5,

We could record the answers like this . . .

input		output
1	→	3
2	→	5
3	→	7
4	→	9
5	→	11

Each input number matches only one output number.
We could record the answers in a table, like this . . .

Input	1	2	3	4	5
Output	3	5	7	9	11

Input each of these numbers: 0, 1, 2, 3, 4, into the function machines and record the outputs in the tables.

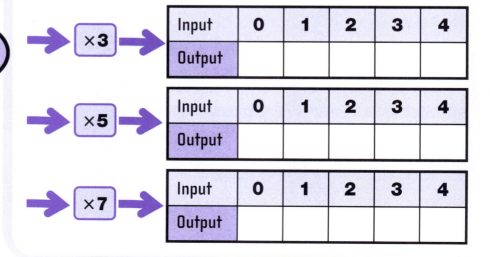

→×3→ Input	0	1	2	3	4
Output					

→×5→ Input	0	1	2	3	4
Output					

→×7→ Input	0	1	2	3	4
Output					

Linear graphs

Functions are sometimes written in a different way.

y = 2x is the same as **× 2**

If we write a function like this using the letters x and y, we can draw a graph . . .

y = 2x

x	0	1	2	3	4
y	0	2	4	6	8

Once we have recorded this in a table we can plot the points on a graph.

These are our coordinates . . . (0, 0) (1, 2) (2, 4) (3, 6) (4, 8)

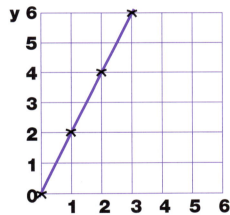

The coordinates can be joined to make a straight line.

This line is called

y = 2x

Examples ▼

Here are some pictures of other functions.

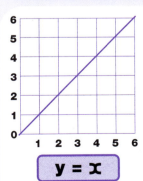

y = x

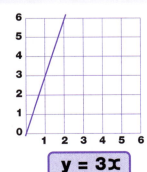

y = 3x

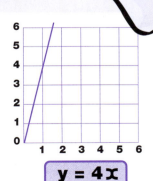

y = 4x

Notice that each line goes through the origin (0, 0).

HELPFUL HINT

Make sure you write the letter x in a different way from the multiplication sign. In maths most people write a 'curly' letter x, like this **x**

Maths words

These straight line graphs are called **linear graphs**. **Linear graphs** are made from functions that have the letters x and y.

See page 40 to learn more about coordinates.

Take a look . . .

Look at how steep the lines on the graphs are:
look first at y = x
then at y = **2**x
then at y = **3**x
and so on.

Can you guess what y = **5**x will look like?

Lines, angles, shapes

★ Geometry

Geometry is the name given to the part of maths that explores lines, shapes and angles. The word Geometry means 'measuring the Earth'. It is similar to Geography, which means 'mapping the Earth' or Geology, which is the 'study of the Earth'.

Angles are measured in degrees, written as °. There are 360° in a full turn, 90° in a right angle and 180° in a half turn.

Maths words

An '**equilateral triangle**' has three equal sides and three equal angles.
An '**isosceles triangle**' has two equal sides and two equal angles.
A '**scalene triangle**' has no equal sides and no equal angles.

4 straight sides
5 straight sides
6 straight sides
7 straight sides
8 straight sides
10 straight sides

This page explores lines, angles and shapes. In these topics there are many new words that you should learn.

When two straight lines are drawn on a flat surface they can intersect, or cross. The point at which they intersect is called the intersection . . .

Where any two straight lines meet an angle is formed. The angle is the amount of turn (rotation) from one line to the other.

When straight lines join to make a closed flat shape we can find its name by looking at the number of sides and its properties.

Which of these shapes could you recognise?

Triangle	– equilateral, isosceles, or scalene
Quadrilateral	– parallelogram, rectangle, square, rhombus, kite, trapezium
Pentagon	– regular or irregular
Hexagon	– regular or irregular
Heptagon	– regular or irregular
Octagon	– regular or irregular
Decagon	– regular or irregular

Angles

When drawing triangles, use the capital letters ABC to mark the corners (vertices)...

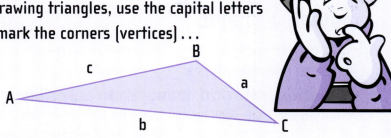

The **sides** of a triangle are called a, b and c (small letters).

The side opposite corner A is called a, the side opposite corner B is called b and the side opposite corner C is called c.

The angles of a triangle are written using the corner letters, like this...

$\hat{ABC}$ means the angle at B
$\hat{BCA}$ means the angle at C
$\hat{CAB}$ means the angle at A

Angle rules to know:

Whenever lines meet at a point the angles add to make 360°

Whenever angles make a straight line the angles add to make 180°

Whenever two lines cross the opposite angles are the same

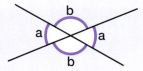

The angles inside any triangle add to make 180°

This is an isosceles triangle as two angles are equal and two sides are equal.

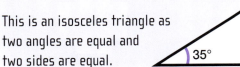

Parallel and perpendicular lines

Lines are **parallel** when they are the same distance apart along their whole length. No matter how long the lines are, they will never meet.

Arrows are used to show that lines are parallel. Lines are **perpendicular** when they are at right angles to each other.

3D shapes

Geometry also includes looking at 3D shapes, such as cubes, cuboids, pyramids, prisms, cylinders, spheres and hemispheres.

How well can you draw pictures of these 3D shapes?

Once you have drawn them, can you work out how many

★ faces
★ vertices
★ edges

each shape has?

Transformations

Watch out for diagonal mirror lines!

Diagonal mirror lines often confuse people, like this . . .

Is this a correct reflection?
Answer: NO!
But this is . . .

Tip: Turn the paper so that the mirror line is vertical. Can you see that it is reflected correctly now?

Maths words

Reflective symmetry is sometimes also called 'refle<u>ct</u>ion symmetry'.

'Rotati<u>on</u>al symmetry' is sometimes also called rotation symmetry.

Transformations are ways of changing or moving a shape.

There are four main types:
reflection, **rotation**, **translation** and **enlargement**.
(In Years **6** and **7** you need to know about the first three types.)

Reflection

To reflect a shape you need a mirror line.
Mirror lines can be vertical, horizontal or diagonal.

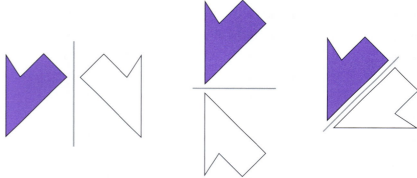

The reflection or new shape is called the image.
When reflecting a shape, take each vertex (corner) at a time. Work out where the reflection of each vertex is and then join up the new points to make the image.

Reflective symmetry

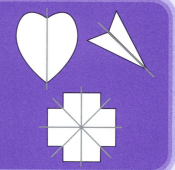

A shape has reflective symmetry when it has one or more lines of symmetry. These shapes all have reflective symmetry.

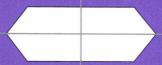

Rotation

To rotate (or turn) a shape you need a centre of rotation.

The centre of rotation can be inside a shape, on the edge of a shape or outside a shape. You also need to know what angle you are rotating the shape through.

These shapes have been rotated through **180°** or half a turn.

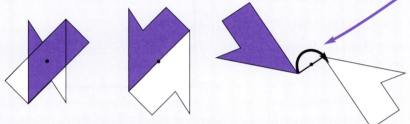

The rotation or new shape is called the image.

When rotating a shape, take each vertex (corner) at a time.
Work out where the rotation of each vertex is and then join up the new points to make the image.

Rotational symmetry

A shape has rotational symmetry when it will fit into its outline as it is turned through **360°**.
These shapes all have rotational symmetry.

order 3   order 5   order 6   order 2

Translation

The third type of transformation you need to know is the easiest!
Translation just means move or slide.
Translations can be horizontal, vertical or diagonal.

Look out!
Make sure you rotate the shape about the centre of rotation, through the correct angle.

Maths words
If the shape has the vertices (corners)
A, B and C,
we call the vertices of the image
A^1, B^1 and C^1.
The number of ways a shape fits into its outline as it is turned through 360° is called the 'order of rotational symmetry'.
We say that a square has the order **4**.

On a grid, diagonal translations are sometimes described as how many across and how many up (or down), like this...
2 to the right, and 1 down

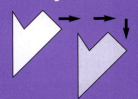

Coordinates

Coordinates...

are given as an 'ordered pair' of numbers, which means that the order in which they are written is important. They are always given in the order

(x, y)

The number on the x (horizontal) axis is given first.

Maths words

The 'origin' on a graph is the point **(0,0)**.
The 'x axis' is horizontal and the 'y axis' is vertical. The plural of axis is **axes**.
A 'quadrant' is a section of a graph. Quadrants are separated by **axes**. There are 4 quadrants.

2nd	1st
3rd	4th

Coordinates are used to pinpoint a position on a map or graph.

The **coordinates** of the house are (**2, 3**).
This means **2** across on the x (horizontal) axis and **3** up on the y (vertical) axis.

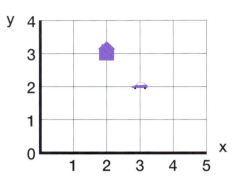

What are the coordinates of the car?

The grid above plots a point in the first quadrant. We can plot points in all four quadrants by extending the axes through the origin, like this...

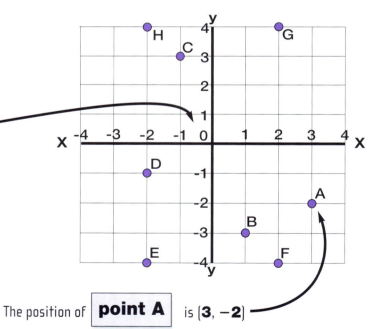

The position of | **point A** | is (**3, −2**)

What are the coordinates of:

| **point B?** | **point C?** | **point D?** |

What letters are at points:

(2, 4)?   **(2, −4)?**   **(−2, 4)?**   **(−2, −4)?**

Try plotting and naming some points of your own.

Working with coordinates

To improve your understanding of coordinates try playing these games with a friend.

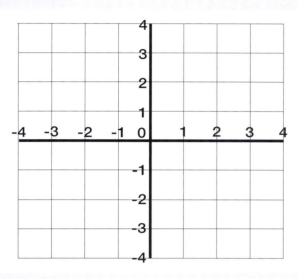

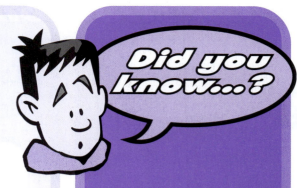

Did you know...?

The system of coordinates shown on these pages was invented by a French mathematician called René Descartes in the 1600s. Because of this they are sometimes known as Cartesian coordinates.

Game **1**
Take turns to name and mark a point in your colour.
The winner is the first player to get a straight line of 4 points in any direction.

Game **2**
Draw a grid with each axis marked from 3 to −3.
Take turns to mark a point on the grid in your own colour.
Carry on until all the points have been marked. Now find four points in your colour that form the corners of a square.
The coordinates of each square must be written down.
The winner is the player who can find most squares.

Try these ...

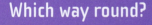

★ Plot the points (3, 1) and (3, 3). These are two of the corners of a rectangle. Write three pairs of coordinates that could, in turn, be the other corners.
★ Plot the vertices of a) a triangle, b) a kite and c) a parallelogram on the grid.
★ Plot the points of a quadrilateral that has a vertex in each quadrant.

Which way round?

If you can't remember which way round to plot coordinates...
★ 'in the house and up (or down) the stairs'
★ 'along the corridor and up (or down) the stairs'
★ 'x is a cross' or
★ 'y is high'

Construction

? **Which tools do you need?**

Make sure you have a sharp pencil, a good ruler marked with millimetres and a protractor.

Your protractor can be a semi-circular or a circular one.

(You might also need a pair of compasses for more difficult construction work.)

⭐ WISE UP

Make sure you read either the outer numbers on the protractor or the inner numbers. Don't mix up both!

Sometimes you need to be able to use the angle you have drawn to make part of a shape, like a triangle.

Construction is the part of maths where you draw lines, angles and shapes accurately, using rulers, protractors and other tools.

Drawing lines

When drawing lines with a ruler, make your lines as accurate as you can. Sharpen your pencil and read the measurement to the nearest millimetre.

Drawing angles

It is important to be able to draw angles accurately using a protractor.

1. Draw a dot to be the point where the lines meet.
2. Put the origin of the protractor on this point.
3. Mark 0 and the angle you want.
4. Join these two marks to the dot using a ruler.

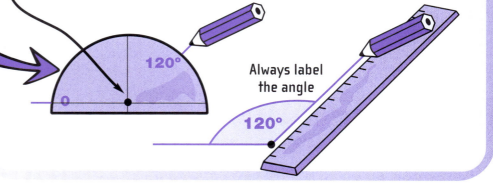

Always label the angle

120°

120°

0

Drawing triangles

Once you can draw angles and lines accurately, you can join them together to make shapes.

Draw a triangle that has an angle of **58°** and two sides that are **7** cm.

Draw the angle first using a protractor.

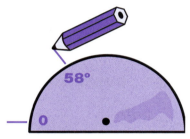

Then measure the two lines with a ruler, making them **7** cm. Now use a ruler to join the two to make a triangle.

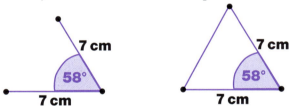

Sometimes you will be asked to measure the third side or the other two angles accurately.

Try it yourself

Draw a triangle that has an angle of **75°** and two sides that are **7** cm.

Use a ruler to find the length of the third side.

Draw a triangle that has an angle of **46°** and two sides that are **8** cm.

Use a protractor to find the other two angles.

Try triangles!
This will be an isosceles triangle because two of its sides are equal.
If all three angles were 60° then the triangle would be equilateral.

See page 36 to learn more about angles and different types of triangles.

Try this . . .
Once you know how to draw triangles when you are given two sides and one angle, you may be asked to draw a triangle when you are given two angles and one side.
Do this in a similar way. Measure one angle and then make one of the lines the length that you've been given. At the other end of this line draw the other angle.
Now the lines should cross.

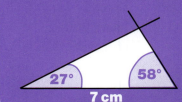

Measurement 1

Maths words

There are two main types of units that we use: metric units and imperial units.

Imperial units such as inches and gallons used to be the only type we used, but now scientists and mathematicians use metric units because they are easier to work with.

A centilitre is one hundredth of a litre. It is the same as **10** millilitres (about a dessert spoon full of liquid).

Where would we be without units?

I'll meet you there in one ...
Can I have 300 ...
of cheese?
I've just run 26 ...

There are many different measurement topics, including length, mass, capacity, area, time, angle, temperature and so on.

Each measurement topic uses a different set of units, such as centimetres or grams.

Here is a list of standard metric units.

millimetre (mm)	**centimetre (cm)**
metre (m)	**kilometre (km)**
gram (g)	**kilogram (kg)**
millilitre (ml)	**centilitre (cl)**
litre (l)	

Do you know which topic each of these units belongs to?

We also use units such as these for measuring temperature, time and angles...

degrees Celsius (°C)
seconds (s)
minutes (min)
hours (h)
degrees (°)

We also use the units
day,
week,
month,
year,
decade,
century and millennium
when describing time.

Because measurements can usually be given using more than one unit, we need to know how to convert (change) from one unit to another.

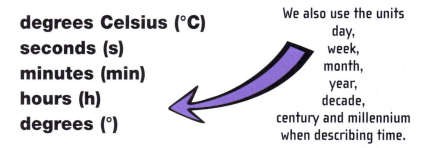

45 cm ⬌ 450 mm ⬌ 0.45 m

Converting between units

When converting from one unit to another you need to know how many of one make up the other.

If you know that $\boxed{100\text{ cm} = 1\text{ m}}$ then you know that:

★ you will multiply the number of metres by **100** to get the number of centimetres.

★ you will divide the number of centimetres by **100** to get the number of metres.

$\boxed{\text{Change }\textbf{4.6}\text{ m to cm}}$ $\textbf{4.6}\text{ m}\ \xrightarrow{\times\ \textbf{100}}\ = \textbf{460}\text{ cm}$

Make sure you can remember how to multiply and divide numbers by 10, 100 and 1000. See page 21.

Try these . . .

Change **88** m to cm	Change **7.5** cm to m
Change **8000** ml to l	Change **150** g to kg
Change **3.4** kg to g	Change **1.75** l to ml

Imperial units

If you are told a measurement using imperial units, you can convert it to metric if you know approximately how many of one unit makes the other.

$\boxed{\textbf{4.5}\text{ litres} \approx \textbf{1}\text{ gallon}}$

| Change **3** gallons to litres | Change **27** litres to gallons |

⭐ Helpful diagrams

It is sometimes easier to use a diagram, like these . . .

$$\times 100$$
$$m \rightleftarrows cm$$
$$\div 100$$

$$\times 1000$$
$$l \rightleftarrows ml$$
$$\div 1000$$

$$\times 1000$$
$$kg \rightleftarrows g$$
$$\div 1000$$

Converting imperial to metric units

$$\times 4.5$$
$$gallon \rightleftarrows l$$
$$\div 4.5$$

Note that when converting between imperial and metric the answer will be an approximation.

Measurement 2

Did you know...?

The area of the United Kingdom is **244 000** km² (square kilometres).

The area of the USA is **9 363 000** km²!

For more about formulae see page 31.

★ Other shapes made using rectangles

Look at these shapes. To find the area of the shaded part you still use the formula for the area of a rectangle. Can you see why?

First find the area of the large rectangle.

Then subtract the areas of the white rectangles.

Other measurement topics include finding the area and perimeter of 2D shapes or the surface area or volume of 3D shapes.

The perimeter of a 2D shape is the distance all the way around the edge of it.

The area of a 2D shape is the amount of surface that it covers.

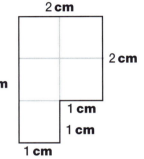

The perimeter of this shape is
$3 + 2 + 2 + 1 + 1 + 1 = 10$ cm

The area of this shape is 5 square centimetres (5 cm²).

Finding the area of a rectangle

Here is the formula for working out the area of a rectangle.

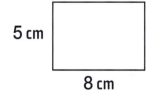

length width
Area = l × w
Area = 8 × 5 = 40 cm²

Compound shapes

Some shapes are made by joining rectangles together. These are sometimes called compound shapes.

To find the area of a compound shape, split it into rectangles, find the area of each and add them together.

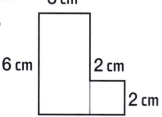

$6 × 3 = 18$ cm² $2 × 2 = 4$ cm²
Total area = 18 + 4 = 22 cm²

3D shapes

When looking at 3D shapes we can measure the **surface area** or the **volume**.

The **surface area** is the area of all the faces added together.

If I cover each face of this cuboid in a rectangle of paper, what area of paper do I need? That's the surface area.

Surface area =
end face $8 \times 10 = 80 \text{ cm}^2$
top/bottom face $20 \times 8 = 160 \text{ cm}^2$
front/back face $20 \times 10 = 200 \text{ cm}^2$

So the two end faces	= 160
Two top and bottom faces	= 320
Two front and back faces	= <u>400</u>
Total surface area	= <u>**880**</u> **cm²**

20 cm
10 cm
8 cm

The volume is the amount of space a 3D shape takes up.
It can be found by seeing how many cubes (cubic centimetres) take up the same space as the shape.

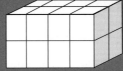

4 cm
2 cm
2 cm

This shape has **2** rows of **4** cubes in each layer.
There are **2** layers. So the volume is **16** cubes (cm³).

Think...
How many faces has a cuboid?
How many of these faces are the same?
Think of the faces in pairs:
The end faces (at each side), the top and bottom faces and then the front and back faces.

Can you work this out?
If a cuboid is made from 6 cubes (6 cm³) what is its surface area?

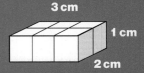

3 cm
1 cm
2 cm

Find the areas of the faces in pairs.

47

Averages

Why do we use averages?

Averages help us to get a sense of what data is telling us.

For example, if United scored 6 goals on Saturday this might be very unusual. To get a sense of how many United typically score it is better to use an average taken over many games.

> If there is no middle value, the median is halfway between the two middle numbers.
> The median of 3, 5, 9, and 10 is 7, because 7 is halfway between 5 and 9.

Maths words

The 'range' is the difference between the highest and lowest values. Find the range by subtracting the smallest from the largest value.
The 'modal group' in a set of data is the most frequent group that occurs – see grouped data on page 50.

Averages are used to represent a middle or typical value in a set of numbers.

There are three types of average:
mean, median and mode.

Let's take some data, like a list of Sara's maths results in the last five tests . . .

Sara's last five scores were | 10 | 2 | 7 | 9 | 2 |

mean
to find the mean we find the total of all Sara's scores and then divide this by the number of scores

$10 + 2 + 7 + 9 + 2 = 30$

$30 \div 5 = 6$

★ the mean is **6**

median
to find the median we put all the scores in order and then find the middle value

2, 2, ⑦, 9, 10
middle value

★ the median is **7**

mode
to find the mode we look for the most popular, or most frequent, value in the list

10, ②, 7, 9, ②

2 is the most frequent value

★ the mode is **2**

Now try this . . .

This table shows the amounts Mr. M. T. Pockets spent in 6 weeks. Find the

★ mean
★ median
★ mode

Work out the range of this set of data.

Week	amount
1	£6
2	£2
3	£19
4	£13
5	£6
6	£8

Working with averages

Here is a set of data where the mean, median and mode all have the same value:

6	9	5	4	6

★ What value are they?

★ Can you create a set of data where they are all the same?

★ Can you create a set of data where they are all different?

This chart shows the daily wages at *Andy's Decorators.*

There are 4 tilers, 3 painters and 1 manager.

Wages	
Manager	£234
Painters	£66
Tilers	£58

The firm is advertising for more tilers and painters.

It says, "Our average daily pay is **£83**".

Which average is being used here?

Is it fair for the firm to say this? Why do you think this?

Which average would have given the answer £62? And £58?

To find the **mode** –	see which is the most common wage.
To find the **median** –	list all the daily wages for each person in order. Then find the middle value.
To find the **mean** –	find the total amount paid to all the staff. **4 × £58, 3 × £66 and 1 × £234** Now divide by the total number of staff.

Look at a list of football results.

Were more goals scored in the first half or second half of the game?

Calculate the mean, median, mode and range for goals scored in each of the halves.

Write a few sentences, using the words mean, median, mode and range, to explain your findings.

Which average to use?

When people talk about 'the average' of something they are usually referring to the mean. But sometimes it is better to use another type of average . . .

A darts player scores 45, 48, 53, 59, 61, 67, 171 and 180

mean = **85.5**

median = **60**

The median gives a better idea of what he is likely to throw.

Average family in Britain?

The mean number of children in a British family is **2.4**.

The mode is perhaps a better average to use in this case.

More families have 2 children than any other number, so the mode is **2**.

Graphs

? Why do we use graphs?

Graphs help us to display information in a way that is clear and more easily understood.

Maths words

'**Grouped data**' is data that has been grouped together to make it easier to show.

A '**class interval**' is the size of the groups we might use when dividing up a set of data.

'**Discrete data**' is information about numbers of things we can count, like the coins in your pocket or the cars in a car park.

The '**frequency**' of an event is the number of times it happens, like the frequency of tossing a coin and getting heads might be 5 out of 10.

Graphs are used to display information in different ways.

There are several types of graph you will meet at secondary school. You will already be familiar with some of them.

Bar charts

This bar chart shows the sizes of shoes worn by a group of **14** year olds. It uses discrete data, grouped data and equal class intervals.

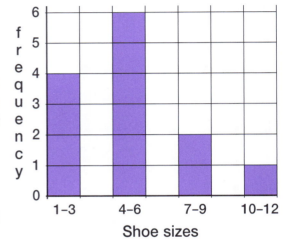

★ The data is grouped to make the graph easier to use. Otherwise there would have to be **12** separate columns to show this data.

★ The size of each group, or class interval, is three shoe sizes.

★ The data is discrete data because it is about things we can count, so all possible shoe sizes can be listed.

★ When we count the number of people wearing size 4 we are finding the frequency with which that size occurs.

Bar line graphs

This bar line graph uses bars to show the frequency with which numbers are rolled on a dice. Here the numbers on the dice are not grouped and so there are no class intervals.

Scores on a dice rolled **100** times

Interpreting graphs

Graphs are only useful to us if we can understand what they are showing.

Being able to 'read' a graph is known as interpreting it. Look at the first graph opposite. The following statements are a result of interpreting the graph...

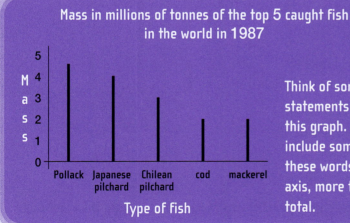

twice as many people wear size **1, 2** or **3** than wear size **7, 8** or **9**

6 people wear size **4, 5** or **6** shoes

Can you think of two more statements we could make?

We can interpret the graph and use it to predict other data.

★ How do you think a graph showing the shoe sizes worn by a group of 16 year olds might be different?

Mass in millions of tonnes of the top 5 caught fish in the world in 1987

	Pollack	Japanese pilchard	Chilean pilchard	cod	mackerel

Mass (5, 4, 3, 2, 1, 0)

Type of fish

Think of some statements about this graph. Try to include some of these words: range, axis, more than, total.

You can collect data to make a graph. Here are some ideas...
★ numbers of goals scored by all the teams in the league
★ the numbers of different birds on the bird table
★ different types of TV programmes in an evening
Could you use grouped data and class intervals?
Afterwards write some statements to interpret the graphs.

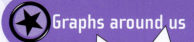

Graphs around us

Graphs are used in real life all the time – on the TV, in adverts, newspapers and magazines. Look for examples of graphs in newspapers and magazines. Can you interpret them? Are any of them misleading? Why do you think this is?

More maths words

In later years in secondary school you will meet **continuous data**. This is different from **discrete data** because you can't count it in the same way. Instead we read the data from scales. Examples of **continuous data** include temperature, height, weight and time.

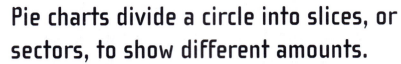

? Why do we use pie charts?

Pie charts are often used to compare sets of data because they display the proportions so clearly. They are only used when there is a small number of sectors to go on the chart, perhaps five or fewer, Otherwise they can look confusing, like this...!

Remember...

The angles in a full turn add up to **360°** (degrees).

For more on proportions see page 18. For more on angles see page 36.

Pie charts divide a circle into slices, or sectors, to show different amounts.

A survey of **36** people to find where they went on holiday last summer:

Country	Number of people
USA	3
Spain	18
Greece	4
Portugal	2
France	9

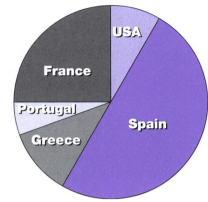

Look at these methods of representing the information – a bar chart and a pie chart.

Each is clear and easy to understand. But the pie chart can give us more information!

Which one is better to answer this question?

What proportion of holidaymakers went to France?

And this question?

Did Spain get a) half b) less than half or c) more than half of all the holidaymakers?

A pie chart is all about angles. It is the size of the angle at the centre of the circle that decides how big each slice, or sector, will be. We use this to answer questions about the pie chart.

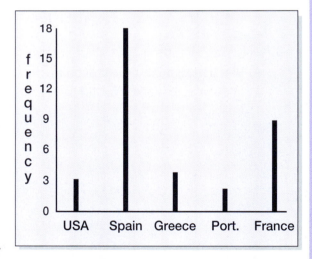

Using pie charts

Look at this pie chart.

The most frequent visitors were house sparrows.

There were about twice as many blackbirds as wrens.

How can we answer this?

How many birds of each type visited the bird table?

We know that there are **360°** in a full turn.

So the **360°** are shared between the **24** birds.

360 ÷ 24 = 15.   So each bird gets **15**°on the chart.

If the angle for blackbirds is **90°**, how many lots of **15**s are in **90**?

Answer: **6** blackbirds.

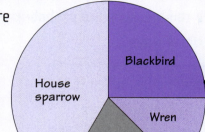

A pie chart showing 24 birds that visited my bird table on Monday

We can also say

'Twenty five per cent were blackbirds'

or

'One quarter of the birds were blackbirds'

Work out how many of each of the other birds came to the table.

Examples ▼

'If the pie chart was showing **72** birds, how many were robins?'

Divide 360° by 72: 360 ÷ 72 = 5.
Each bird on the pie chart gets **5°**.
We know that robins have 75° on the chart, so there must be 15 robins, because 75 ÷ 5 is 15.
Answer: **15 robins**

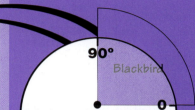

? How to measure?
Use an angle measurer or protractor to measure the angles at the centre.
Blackbird

We can use fractions and percentages to write about what we have found.

For more on fractions and percentages see pages 12 and 16.

Probability 1

Maths words

'Event' is the word used to describe something that has happened or might happen, such as it raining today or United winning on Saturday.

An 'outcome' is the result of something happening. Whether it will rain or not today has two outcomes and picking a day of the week at random has seven outcomes.

'Equally likely outcomes' means that all the possible outcomes of an event are equal. For example, when we roll a dice there are six equally likely outcomes.

Think

'What are the possible outcomes?'

Are they equally likely?

Probability is about the chance, or likelihood, of something happening.

We can measure the probability of something happening in several ways . . .

. . . seeing how often it has happened before
To find the probability of it snowing at Christmas we can find out how often it has happened in the past.
When we know this we can estimate the likelihood of a white Christmas. We might say, in our opinion, it is 'unlikely' or 'very unlikely'.

. . . by doing an experiment
To find the probability of throwing a total of 7 with two dice, we could throw two dice lots of times and record our results.
The more times we throw the dice the more accurate our result will be.
This experiment will help us to estimate the likelihood of scoring 7.

Another is to use the idea of equally likely outcomes.

. . . using equally likely outcomes
To work out the probability of picking a heart at random from a pack of cards we first find out what the possible outcomes are. They are heart, diamond, club or spade.
So there are four outcomes and, because there are 13 cards in each suit, each of these outcomes is equally likely.
So the probability of picking a heart is 1 out of 4 or $\frac{1}{4}$.

Which of these events have equally likely outcomes?
a) A day of the week, picked at random, starting with the letter T.
b) Rolling an even number on a dice.

Working with probability

What are the possible outcomes when, at random,

★ a card is picked from a pack of cards?
There are 52 outcomes and the probability of each is 1/52.

★ an ace is picked from a pack of cards?
There are 52 outcomes, 4 of which are aces, and so the probability of an ace is 4/52 or 1/13.

★ a month of the year beginning with J is picked?
There are 12 outcomes, 3 of which begin with J, and so the probability is 3/12 or 1/4.

Probabilities are often marked on a scale from **0–1**.
We can mark probabilities that have equally likely outcomes on this line, like this one for rolling a dice . . .

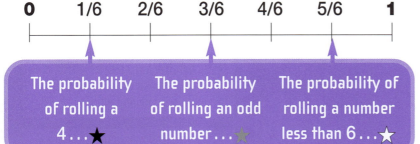

| 0 | 1/6 | 2/6 | 3/6 | 4/6 | 5/6 | 1 |

The probability of rolling a 4 . . . ★

The probability of rolling an odd number . . . ★

The probability of rolling a number less than 6 . . . ☆

★ is 1 out of 6 because there are six equally likely outcomes and rolling a 4 is one of them
★ is 3 out of 6 because there are six equally likely outcomes and 3 of them are odd
☆ is 5 out of 6 because there are six equally likely outcomes and 5 of them are less than 6

What is the probability of rolling
★ a zero?   ★ a six?   ★ a number exactly divisible by 3?
★ a number between 0 and 7?

Where should we mark these probabilities on the scale?

Remember . . .

0 means an event is impossible and **1** means that it is certain. Saying **1** out of **6** or **3** out of **4** is the same as the probabilities 1/6 or 3/4.

Other words we might use when talking about probability include likely, unlikely, even chance, and evens.

? Did you know . . . ?
Weather forecasting is based on probability. Forecasters look at the weather patterns around the world and predict the likelihood of certain types of weather happening. They do this by seeing what has happened before in similar situations.

Probability 2

Did you know...?

The probability of each ticket winning the jackpot on the lottery is about 1 out of 14 000 000!

This is because there are about 14 000 000 possible outcomes.

Each outcome is one combination of six numbers from 1 to 49.

You are just as likely to win with the numbers

1 2 3 4 5 6

as you are with any other combination.

What if the word was MISSISSIPPI?

Probability is about the chance, or likelihood, of something happening.

We have seen how it is possible to measure the probability of something happening by using equally likely outcomes.

The 8 letters of the word BUTTERED are put in a bag and a letter is taken out at random.

★ How many possible outcomes are there?
There are 6 possible outcomes. They are B, U, T, E, R and D.

★ Are these outcomes equally likely?
No, because the chances of getting a T or an E are greater than each of the other letters.

★ What are the probabilities of each of these outcomes?

letter	probability	The probability of picking...
B	1/8	
U	1/8	
T	2/8 or 1/4	
E	2/8 or 1/4	
R	1/8	
D	1/8	

... a B is **1/8** because there are **8** letters in the bag, one of which is B. So the chance of a B is one out of eight.

... a T is **2/8** because there are **8** letters in the bag, two of which are T. So the chance of a T is two out of eight.

If the letters from the word ISOSCELES were put in a bag and a letter is taken out at random:
★ how many outcomes would there be?
★ would they be equally likely?
★ what would be the probabilities of each of these outcomes?

Working with probability

We have seen how it is possible to measure the probability of something happening by doing an experiment.
Let's try one . . .

Dice scores

.	2	3	4	5	6	7
:	3	4	5	6	7	8
∴	4	5	6	7	8	9
::	5	6	7	8	9	10
⁙	6	7	8	9	10	11
⁞⁞	7	8	9	10	11	12

The table shows all the possible scores when two dice are rolled.
Try these questions before looking at the answers at the side.

★ How many outcomes are there?
★ Are they all equally likely?
★ Which score is most likely?
★ Which score has a probability of **1/6**?
★ What is the probability of getting the same number on both dice?

Try this experiment

Write the numbers from **2** to **12** at the top of a sheet of squared paper. Roll two dice, find the total and put a cross under that number. Keep going. Which number do you think will reach the bottom of the sheet first? Does it?

2	3	4	5	6	7	8	9	10	11	12
	X	X		X	X		X			
		X		X	X					
				X						

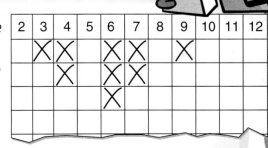

Answers

★ There are 11 possible outcomes.
  These are 2, 3, 4, 5, 6, 7, 8, 9, 10, 11 and 12.
★ No, because there are more ways to roll some of the outcomes, such as 7 or 8, than others, such as 2 or 3.
★ 7, because there are 6 ways of rolling 7.
★ 7, because 6 out of 36 outcomes roll 7. This is 6/36 or 1/6.
★ 6/36 or 1/6, because there are 6 out of 36 ways for this to happen.

Glossary

adjacent means 'next to'.

approximate means an answer that is not exact but very close to the accurate answer. To approximate an answer is to simplify and then work out the calculation.

ascending sequences are those where the terms in the sequence get larger.

averages are used to give us a sense of a set of data. The average value is the most typical or middle value of a set of numbers.

BODMAS – see page 24.

To **calculate** means to work something out.

A **class interval** is the size of the groups we might use when dividing up a set of data.

collecting like terms is a method of simplifying expressions by collecting all the letters together. For example to simplify 4a + 3b − a + 2b we collect the a's and b's to get 3a + 5b.

compound shapes are made from two or more rectangles. To find the area of a compound shape, calculate the areas of the rectangles and add them together.

construction is the part of maths where you draw lines, angles and shapes accurately, using rulers, protractors and other tools.

continuous data is data that may not have an exact value, for example time and temperature. As a result it is treated differently from discrete data.

converting means changing something from one form to another, like changing percentages to fractions or decimals.

coordinates are two numbers corresponding to the position of a point or object. The first number relates to its horizontal position, the second number to its vertical position.

decimals are not whole numbers. They include amounts that are less than one – amounts that can also be written as fractions.

decimal places are the number of digits after the decimal point.

The **decimal point** is the dot separating the whole numbers from the part numbers in a decimal.

The **denominator** is the number at the bottom of a fraction. It shows how many equal parts the whole has been split into.

descending sequences are those where the terms in the sequence get smaller.

discrete data is information about numbers of things we can count, like the coins in your pocket or the cars in a car park.

enlargement is to make the shape bigger.

equally likely outcomes means that the possible outcomes of an event are all equally likely to happen. For example, when we roll a dice there are 6 equally likely outcomes.

equations are number sentences that have an equals sign, such as y + 3 = 6.

An **equilateral triangle** has three equal sides and three equal angles.

equivalent fractions are fractions with the same value even though they have different numerators (top numbers) and denominators (bottom numbers).

An event is anything that has a probability of happening.

expressions do not have an equals sign, such as y + 3.

factors are whole numbers that divide exactly into another number without a remainder.

The frequency of an event is the number of times it happens, like the frequency of tossing a coin and getting heads might be 5 out of 10.

functions are mathematical rules that can be applied to a set of numbers.

grouped data is data that has been grouped together to make it easier to show.

An image is the result of a transformation. For example, if a shape is reflected, the resulting shape is its image.

infinity is greater than any countable number and if a series carries on until infinity it will continue forever.

intersection is the point where two lines meet.

An isosceles triangle has two equal sides and two equal angles.

linear graphs are graphs with a straight line joining the points together.

mean is a type of average. To find the mean we find the total of all the values and then divide this by the number of values.

median is a type of average. To find the median we put all the values in order and then find the middle value.

The modal group is the group of values that most frequently occur in a set of data.

mode is a type of average. To find the mode we look for the most popular, or frequent, value in the list.

A multiple of a number is any number into which it will divide exactly, without a remainder.

negative numbers are numbers less than zero, such as −4, −6.4, −8.333 and −19.

negative numbers and positive numbers together are sometimes called directed numbers.

The numerator is the number on top of a fraction. It shows how many equal parts (the denominator) there are.

The origin on a graph is the point (0,0).

An outcome is the result of something happening. Whether it will rain or not today has two possible outcomes and picking a day of the week at random has seven possible outcomes.

Lines are parallel when they are the same distance apart along their whole length. No matter how long the lines are they will never meet.

partitioning is when a number is split into two parts to make it easier to do calculations.

per cent means 'out of every hundred' or 'for every hundred'.

A percentage is a fraction with a denominator of 100, but written in a different way, using the sign %.

Lines are perpendicular when they are at right angles to each other.

positive numbers are the numbers we normally use all the time, such as 4, 27 and 169. We *could* write them with a plus sign in front like this +4, +27, +169, but we don't usually need to.

We use rules to predict the value of a certain term in a sequence. We can also use graphs to predict data and results.

prime numbers are whole numbers that have only two factors, the number itself and 1, e.g. 2, 5, 11, 31.

probability is about the chance, or likelihood, of something happening.

The product is the result of multiplying numbers together.

proportion is the relationship between part of something and the whole thing. It compares 'part with whole'.

range is the difference between the highest and lowest values. We find the range by subtracting the smallest from the largest value.

ratio is the relationship between two or more numbers or quantities. It compares 'part with part'.

reflection is to reflect a shape in a mirror line.

A shape has reflective symmetry if it has one or more lines of symmetry, meaning that if one side of the shape is reflected into the line of symmetry the image lies exactly over the other side of the shape.

rotation is to rotate or turn a shape.

A shape has rotational symmetry when it will fit onto its outline as it is rotated. The number of times it does so in 360° gives its order of rotational symmetry.

rounding is used to give a less exact, more approximate number.

A scalene triangle has no equal sides and no equal angles.

sequences are numbers arranged in a special order. Each number in a sequence is called a term.

The simplest form of a fraction is when the numerator and denominator have been divided by the largest number possible and cannot be divided down any further.

When we simplify in algebra we collect together letters that are the same. This is sometimes called 'collecting like terms'.

square numbers are any numbers that have been made by multiplying a number with itself once. 1, 4, 9, 16, 25, 36, 49, 64, 81, 100 are all square numbers.

The square root gives us the number that has been multiplied by itself to give a square number.

substitute in algebra is when a number replaces a letter to make the calculation solvable.

The surface area is the area of all the faces of a shape added together.

A term is one of the numbers in a sequence – the first term is the first number, the second term is the second number etc.

transformations are ways of changing or moving a shape.

There are four main types of transformations: reflection, rotation, translation and enlargement.

translation is to move the shape.

volume is the amount of space a three dimensional shape takes up. It is calculated by multiplying the length by the width by the height.

The x axis is the horizontal line on a graph and the y axis is the vertical one. The plural of axis is axes.

Answers

Rounding (page 6)
Try it yourself

36840	36800	37000
76730	76700	77000
45970	46000	46000
5748550	5748600	5749000
9409850	9409900	9410000
2659970	2660000	2660000

Negative numbers (page 8)
Fill in the signs

<	>	>
<	<	<
>	<	>

Adding

3	−5	5
3	3	10

Subtracting

−8	−4	−7
−4	−9	−10

Try it yourself

−4	4	9
−5	−9	−8
−6	−5	−2

Squares, roots and primes (page 10)
Find the answers to these questions

25	16	
36	64	81

Try it yourself

801   1, 3, 9
144   1, 2, 3, 4, 6, 8, 9
31   1
120   1, 2, 3, 4, 5, 6, 8, 10

31 is a prime number. 144 is a square number.

Fractions (page 12)
Try it yourself

$$\frac{3}{9} \qquad \frac{8}{16} \qquad \frac{8}{10}$$
$$\frac{1}{3} \qquad \frac{1}{2} \qquad \frac{1}{3}$$

Now try adding and subtracting

$$\frac{5}{7} \qquad \frac{6}{10} = \frac{3}{5}$$

$$\frac{7}{8} \qquad \frac{1}{10}$$
$$\frac{7}{9} \qquad \frac{7}{15}$$

Decimals (page 14)
Fill in the missing numbers

$$\frac{3}{10} \qquad \frac{4}{100} \qquad \frac{47}{100}$$

$$\frac{5}{10} = \frac{1}{2} \qquad \frac{25}{100} = \frac{1}{4} \qquad 6\frac{41}{100}$$

Put these in order

0.4821   0.576   0.58   0.581   0.6

Try it yourself

0.7806   0.836   0.84   0.841   0.9

Percentages (page 16)
Try answering these questions

60	75	18
96	120	18

Try these...

40%	40%	42%	20%	24%	25%
40%	36%	35%	80%	76%	85%

Ratio and proportion (page 18)
Simplify these ratios

5 : 1	5 : 1	2 : 1	5 : 1
4 : 1	2 : 1	5 : 1	3 : 1

Choc crispies

$$\frac{6}{7} \qquad 6 : 1$$

Raspberry jam

$$\frac{2}{3} \qquad 2 : 1$$

Blackcurrant drink

$$\frac{5}{6} \qquad 5 : 1$$

Try this ...

1400 m

Number facts (page 20)

Doubles – Test Yourself
52   74   98   148   7.8   9.0   14.4   1.08   1.26   0.76   960
1300   1580   9200   16400   188000

Halves – Test Yourself
26   42   48   34   4.1   3.4   3.7   0.44   0.46   0.38   240
320   390   2300   4100   47000

Try it yourself

9   8   7

8   7   6

9   9   9

Calculations 1 (page 22)

Puzzle

1	6	9		1
0		3		2
1	2	8	4	
	6		5	0
4	2	0	9	

Try these . . .
52   0.52   520   0.052   5200   0.0052
0.4   0.004   4   0.0004   40   0.00004

Calculations 2 (page 24)

Try these . . .
1) 21   2) 2   3) 27   4) 18

Using a calculator
1) 8.2   2) 13   3) 3.2   4) 42.33 or 42⅓

Solving problems (page 26)

Puzzles
1) From left, clockwise: 5, 7, 8 and 5
2) 4   5   6   3
    7   8
        2   9   1
3) 24

Algebra 1 (page 28)

Symbols
3   7   2

Letters
$y = 3$ $b = 3$ $c = 36$

Try it yourself
Your answer will be the same as the first number you thought of . . . because we add 5 then take 5 away.
$n + 2 + 3 - 4 - 1$

Algebra 2 (page 30)

Try these. . .
$6g$ $6y + 7$
1 $4f + 8$ b^3

Try it yourself
9   15   7
5   3   7
2   6   14

Sequences (page 32)

Try these . . .
5, 9, 13, 17, 21 . . .   1, 6, 11, 16, 21 . . .
3, 5, 7, 9, 11. . .   4, 9, 14, 19, 24 . . .
The 100th terms will be   401, 496, 201 and 499

Functions (page 34)

Guess the function!
$+3$ $\times 4$ -1

Input and output
0, 3, 6, 9, 12   0, 5, 10, 15, 20   0, 7, 14, 21, 28

Coordinates (page 40)

Car = (3, 2)
B = (1, −3)
C = (−1, 3)
D = (−2, −1)
The letters are G, F, H, E.

Construction (page 42)

Try it yourself
Approximately 8.5 cm.
Angles both 67°.

Measurement 1 (page 44)

Try these . . .
8800 cm   0.075 m
8 l   0.15 kg
3400 g   1750 ml

Imperial units
13.5 litres   6 gallons

Measurement 2

Can you work this out?
22 cm²

Averages (page 48)

Now try this . . .

Mean **£9**   Median **£7**   Mode **£6**   Range **£17**

Working with averages

The value is 6

Andy's decorators

£83 is the mean wage. This is unfair as the mean takes into account the manager's much higher wage and does not reflect the daily wage of the tilers and painters.

£62 is the median.   **£58** is the mode.

Pie charts (page 52)

Using pie charts

Wren = **3**   House Sparrow = **10**   Robin = **5**

Probability 1 (page 54)

Equally likely outcomes

Event **b** has two equally likely outcomes: even number and odd number. Event **a** does not have equally likely outcomes as 2 out of 7 days start with T.

What is the probability of rolling . . .?

A zero? **0**   A six? **1/6**

A number divisible by 3? **2/6 or 1/3**

A number between 0 and 7? **1**

Probability 2 (page 56)

ISOSCELES

6 outcomes

No. Not equally likely.

I = **1/9**

S = **1/3**

O = **1/9**

C = **1/9**

E = **2/9**

L = **1/9**

Timetable

Time	Monday	Tuesday	Wednesday	Thursday	Friday
B R E A K T I M E					
L U N C H T I M E					
B R E A K T I M E					

Notes